Contents

AGES 6–7
NUMERACY

Test 1 Read and write numbers to 100

Use these numbers to help you.

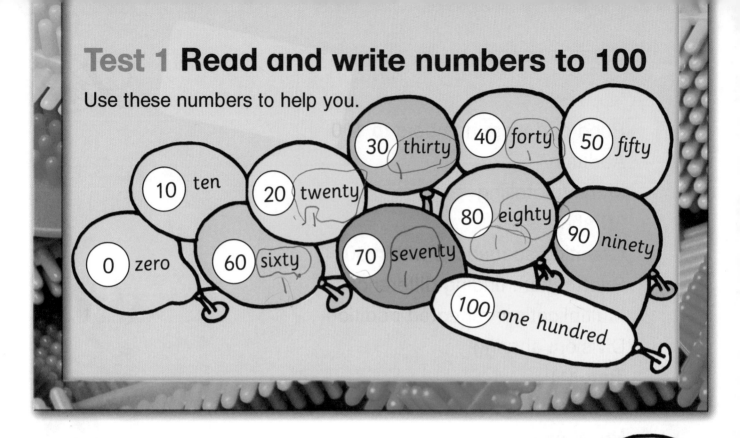

Write the numbers to match the words.

1. thirty-four `34`

2. forty-six `46`

3. twenty-eight `28`

4. seventy-two `72`

5. eighty-nine `89`

Write these numbers as words.

6. 23 twenty three

7. 56 fifty six

8. 91 ninety one

9. 67 sixty seven

10. 49 forty nine

Colour in your score

Test 1

Test 2 Addition

We use a **number line** to help us **add on**.

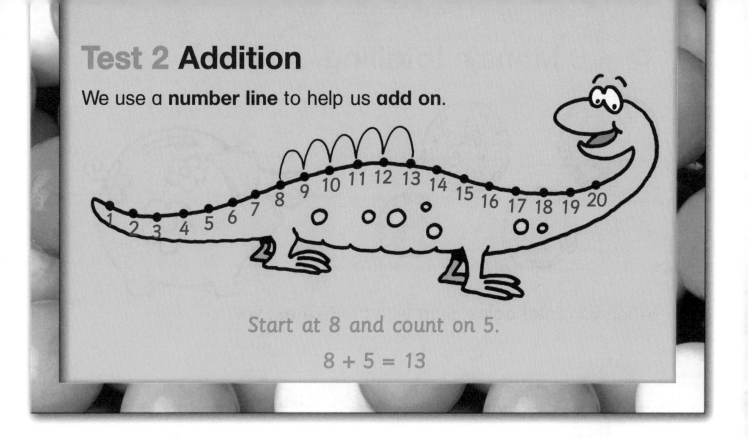

Start at 8 and count on 5.

8 + 5 = 13

Use the number line to help you work out the answers.

1.   6 + 5 =

2.   11 + 3 =

3.   8 + 6 =

4.   12 + 4 =

5.   9 + 5 =

6.   6 + 11 =

7.   7 + 9 =

8.   8 + 4 =

9.   14 + 4 =

10. 13 + 6 =

Colour in your score

Test 2

Test 3 Money: totalling

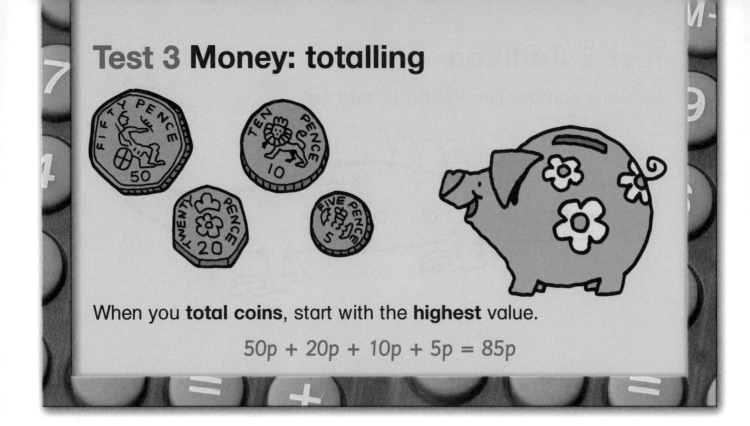

When you **total coins**, start with the **highest** value.

$$50p + 20p + 10p + 5p = 85p$$

Total each set of coins.

1. (10p) (50p) (2p) ⇨ [   ] p

2. (5p) (2p) (2p) (10p) ⇨ [   ] p

3. (2p) (1p) (20p) (10p) ⇨ [   ] p

4. (20p) (10p) (50p) (2p) ⇨ [   ] p

5. (2p) (5p) (10p) (1p) ⇨ [   ] p

6. (50p) (20p) (2p) (1p) ⇨ [   ] p

7. (20p) (20p) (2p) (10p) (2p) ⇨ [   ] p

8. (2p) (1p) (10p) (5p) (10p) ⇨ [   ] p

9. (50p) (20p) (5p) (10p) (1p) ⇨ [   ] p

10. (2p) (10p) (2p) (5p) (20p) ⇨ [   ] p

Colour in your score

Test 3

Test 4 2D shapes

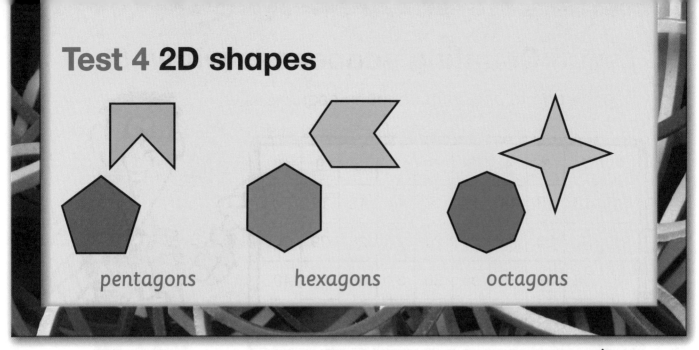

pentagons   hexagons   octagons

Answer these questions.

1. All triangles have ☐ sides.

2. All hexagons have ☐ sides.

3. All pentagons have ☐ sides.

4. All octagons have ☐ sides.

5. All quadrilaterals have ☐ sides.

Name these shapes.

6. _____

7. _____

8. _____

9. _____

10. _____

10
9
8
7
6
5
4
3
2
1

Colour in your score

Test 4

Test 5 Counting sequences within 50

Use the grid to help with counting sequences.

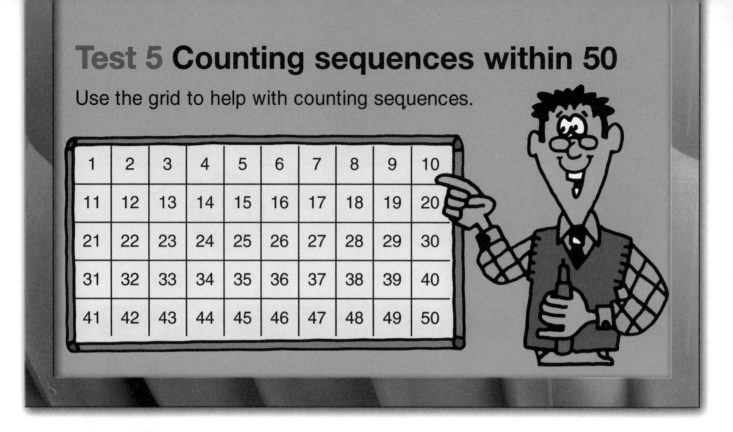

1	2	3	4	5	6	7	8	9	10
11	12	13	14	15	16	17	18	19	20
21	22	23	24	25	26	27	28	29	30
31	32	33	34	35	36	37	38	39	40
41	42	43	44	45	46	47	48	49	50

Write the missing number in each sequence.

1. 24 25 26 ◯ 28 29

2. 35 36 37 38 ☐ 40

3. ☐ 19 20 21 22 23

4. 41 ☐ 43 44 45 46

5. 28 29 30 31 32 ◯

6. 43 42 41 ☐ 39 38

7. 29 28 ☐ 26 25 24

8. 18 ☐ 16 15 14 13

9. 47 46 45 44 ◯ 42

10. ☐ 39 38 37 36 35

Colour in your score

Test 5

Test 6 Subtraction: finding differences

Counting in jumps can help to find the difference.

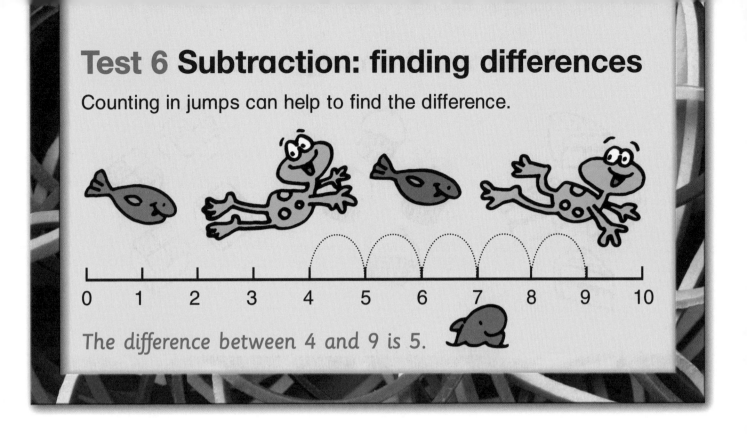

The difference between 4 and 9 is 5.

Write the differences between these pairs of numbers.

1.   ☐   6.   ☐

2.   ☐   7.   ☐

3. ☐   8.   ☐

4. ☐   9.   ☐

5.  ☐   10.  ☐

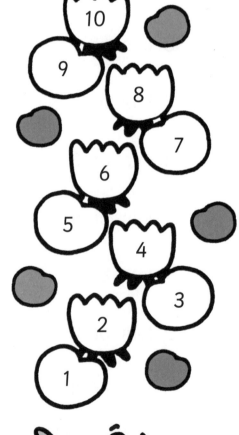

Colour in your score

Test 7 Multiplication: repeated addition

3 lots of 4 is 12

Write the answers.

1. 3 lots of 2 ➪ b
2. 2 lots of 4 ➪ 8
3. 3 lots of 3 ➪ 9
4. 2 lots of 5 ➪ 10
5. 4 lots of 3 ➪
6. 2 lots of 2 ➪
7. 5 lots of 3 ➪
8. 3 lots of 5 ➪
9. 4 lots of 2 ➪
10. 2 lots of 3 ➪

Colour in your score

Test 7

Test 8 Division: sharing

These sweets are shared equally.

15 sweets among 3 children ⇨ 5 each.

Write the answers.

1. 12 shared by 2 ⇨ 14

2. 8 shared by 4 ⇨ 12

3. 6 shared by 3 ⇨

4. 10 shared by 2 ⇨

5. 9 shared by 3 ⇨

6. 12 shared by 3 ⇨

7. 10 shared by 5 ⇨

8. 6 shared by 2 ⇨

9. 12 shared by 4 ⇨

10. 8 shared by 2 ⇨

10
9
8
7
6
5
4
3
2
1

Colour in your score

Test 9 Time (1)

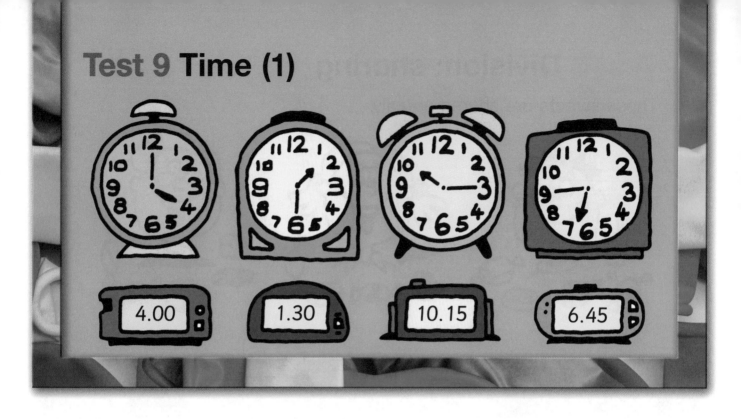

4.00   1.30   10.15   6.45

Write the times for each clock.
Choose from these times.

1.15	3.30	4.45	8.00	2.30
8.45	3.15	7.30	9.00	4.15

1. 

2. 

3. 

4. 

5. 

6. 

7. 

8. 

9. 

10. 

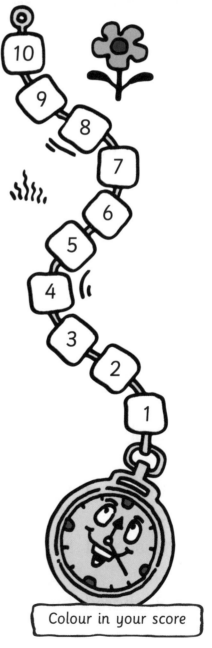

Colour in your score

Test 9

Test 10 Data: block graphs

Colour this **graph** showing the favourite fruit of a group of children.

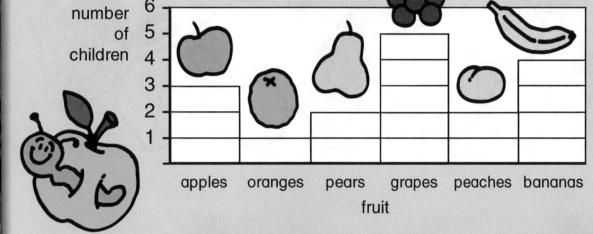

How many children chose:

1. oranges? ☐

2. grapes? ☐

3. bananas? ☐

4. peaches? ☐

5. Which fruit was the children's favourite? ☐

6. Which fruit was chosen by 3 children? ☐

7. How many more children chose grapes than peaches? ☐

8. How many fewer children chose oranges than bananas? ☐

9. How many children chose pears and peaches altogether? ☐

10. How many children were there altogether? ☐

Test 11 Breaking up numbers

$$30 + 7 = 37$$

$$20 + 4 = 24$$

Write the missing numbers.

1.   43   =   ☐   +   3

2.   56   =   50   +   ☐

3.   39   =   30   +   ☐

4.   61   =   ☐   +   1

5.   27   =   ☐   +   7

6.   46   =   40   +   ☐

7.   83   =   ☐   +   3

8.   74   =   ☐   +   4

9.   32   =   30   +   ☐

10.   91   =   ☐   +   1

Colour in your score

Test 11

Test 12 Subtraction facts

This is a **function machine** for changing numbers.

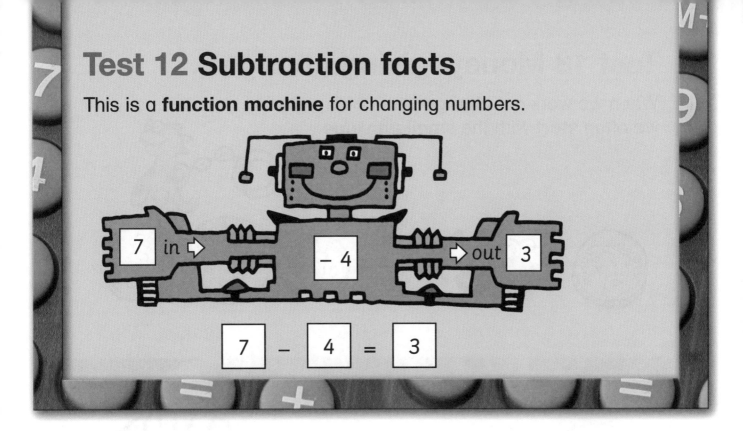

$$7 \quad - \quad 4 \quad = \quad 3$$

Write the missing numbers.

1. 8 − ☐ = 5

2. ☐ − 2 = 6

3. 7 − 3 = ☐

4. ☐ − 4 = 5

5. 9 − ☐ = 6

6. 8 − 2 = ☐

7. ☐ − 3 = 7

8. 8 − ☐ = 3

9. 6 − ☐ = 1

10. ☐ − 4 = 3

Colour in your score

Test 12

Test 13 Money: giving change

When we work out **change** with **coins**,
we often **start** with the **smallest value**.

65p

change: 35p

£1 is given for each toy. Write the change given.

1.   85p   [ ] p

2.   70p   [ ] p

3.   55p   [ ] p

4.   60p   [ ] p

5.   80p   [ ] p

6.   45p   [ ] p

7.   75p   [ ] p

8.   89p   [ ] p

9.   78p   [ ] p

10. 67p   [ ] p

10
9
8
7
6
5
4
3
2
1

Colour in your score

Test 14 3D shapes

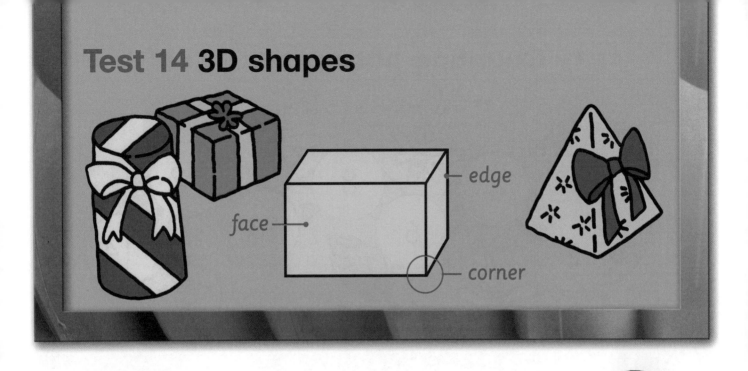

face — edge
corner

Name these shapes.

1. _____

4. _____

2. _____

5. _____

3. 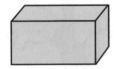 _____

6. _____

How many faces have each of these shapes?

7. ☐ faces

9. ☐ faces

8. ☐ faces

10. ☐ faces

Colour in your score

Test 14

Test 15 Counting patterns

Write the next number in the pattern.

1. 18 20 22 24 26 ◯

2. 34 36 38 40 42 ☐

3. 20 25 30 35 40 ◯

4. 15 18 21 24 27 ☐

5. 8 12 16 20 24 ◯

Write the missing number.

6. 14 — ☐ — 18 — 20 — 22 — 24

7. 45 — 40 — 35 — ☐ — 25 — 20

8. 9 — 12 — ☐ — 18 — 21 — 24

9. 28 — 24 — 20 — 16 — ☐ — 8

10. ☐ — 27 — 24 — 21 — 18 — 15

Colour in your score

Test 15

Test 16 Decade sums

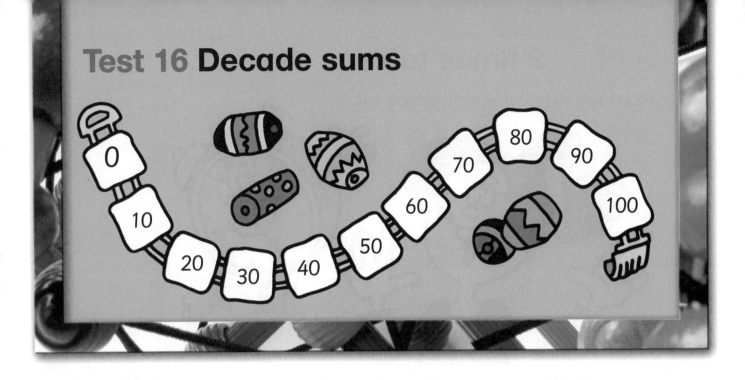

Answer these questions.

1. 40 + 20 = ☐

2. 30 + 30 = ☐

3. 30 + 10 = ☐

4. 40 + 60 = ☐

5. 50 + 40 = ☐

6. 20 + 20 = ☐

The three corner numbers add up to 100.
Write the missing number.

7.
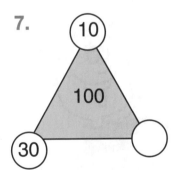
10 — 100 — 30 — ○

8.
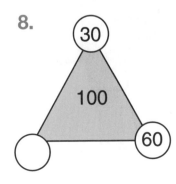
30 — 100 — ○ — 60

9.
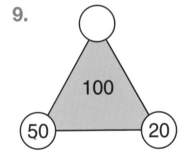
○ — 100 — 50 — 20

10.
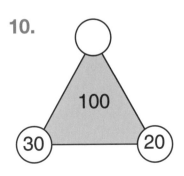
○ — 100 — 30 — 20

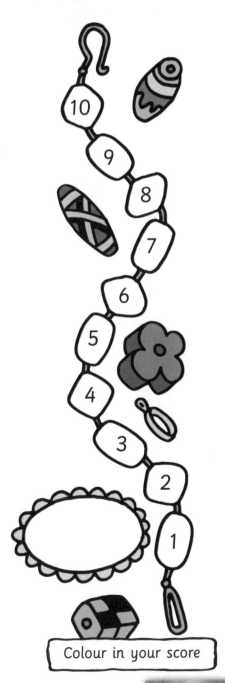

Colour in your score

Test 16

Test 17 2 times table

You need to know your **2 times table**.

How quickly can you answer these?

1. $3 \times 2 =$ ☐

2. $7 \times 2 =$ ☐

3. $2 \times 6 =$ ☐

4. $8 \times 2 =$ ☐

5. $2 \times 4 =$ ☐

6. $2 \times 9 =$ ☐

7. $5 \times 2 =$ ☐

8. $1 \times 2 =$ ☐

9. $10 \times 2 =$ ☐

10. $2 \times 2 =$ ☐

Colour in your score

Test 17

Test 18 Fractions: halves and quarters

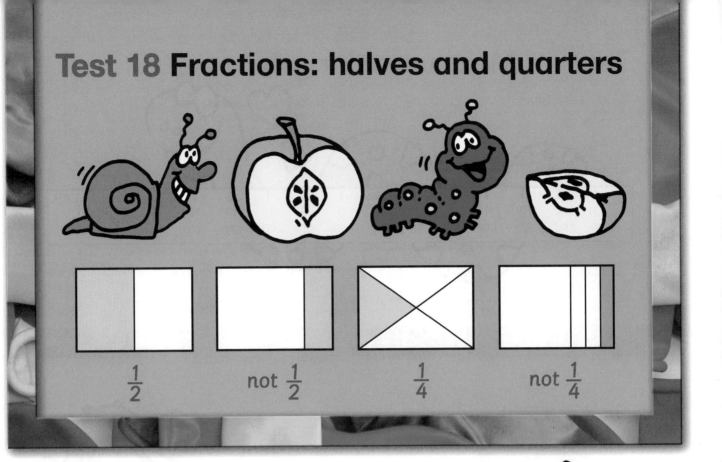

$\frac{1}{2}$ not $\frac{1}{2}$ $\frac{1}{4}$ not $\frac{1}{4}$

Colour $\frac{1}{2}$ of each shape.   **Colour $\frac{1}{4}$ of each shape.**

1.

2.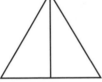

3.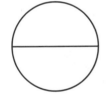

4.

5.

6.

7.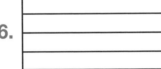

8.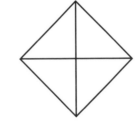

9.

10.

10
9
8
7
6
5
4
3
2
1

Colour in your score

Test 18

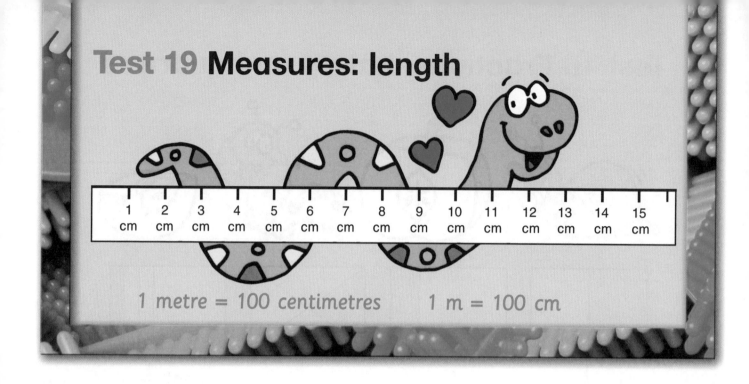

Test 19 Measures: length

1 metre = 100 centimetres   1 m = 100 cm

Measure these lines.

1. _____ ☐ cm

2. _____ ☐ cm

3. _____ ☐ cm

4. _____ ☐ cm

5. _____ ☐ cm

Guess how long each worm is.

6. ☐ cm

7. ☐ cm

8. ☐ cm

9. ☐ cm

10. ☐ cm

Colour in your score

Test 19

Test 20 Data: pictograms

This **pictogram** shows the pets owned by a group of children.

dogs	🐕 🐕 🐕 🐕 🐕
cats	🐱 🐱 🐱 🐱 🐱 🐱
rabbits	🐰 🐰 🐰
mice	🐭 🐭 🐭
fish	🐟 🐟 🐟 🐟

How many children have a pet:

1. dog

2. fish

3. mouse

4. rabbit

5. cat

6. How many more cats are there than fish ?

7. How many fewer rabbits are there than dogs?

8. How many mice and cats are there altogether?

9. How many fish and dogs are there altogether?

10. How many pets are there altogether?

Colour in your score

Test 20

Test 21 Comparing and ordering numbers

Use this **number line** to help you **compare** and **order numbers**.

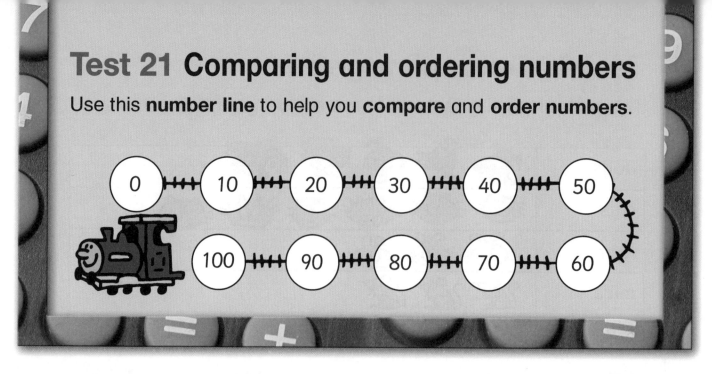

Circle the bigger number in each pair.

1. 46   (61)

2. 68   (83)

3. 39   (41)

4. (93)   39

5. (57)   54

Write the numbers in order starting with the smallest.

6. 18 34 27 41

7. 61 52 59 62

8. 38 41 52 37

9. 51 53 59 54

10. 72 69 64 70

Colour in your score

Test 21

Test 22 Addition and subtraction

This **number trio** makes **addition** and **subtraction** facts.

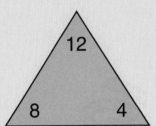

8 + 4 = 12
4 + 8 = 12

12 − 4 = 8
12 − 8 = 4

Write the addition and subtraction facts for each of these number trios.

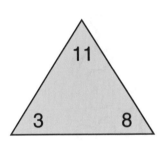

3 + 8 = 11

8 + 3 = 11

1. 11 − ☐ = 8

2. 11 − 8 = ☐

3. 8 + ☐ = 14

4. 6 + ☐ = ☐

5. ☐ − 6 = ☐

6. ☐ − 8 = ☐

7. ☐ + 7 = ☐

8. ☐ + 9 = ☐

9. 16 − ☐ = ☐

10. ☐ − ☐ = 7

Colour in your score

Test 22

Test 23 Problems

To work out a **missing number** use the other numbers to help you.

$$\boxed{} + 6 = 15$$

Something add 6 equals 15.

$$9 + 6 = 15$$

Write the missing numbers.

1. $\boxed{} + 3 = 11$

2. $6 + \boxed{} = 12$

3. $\boxed{} + 7 = 15$

4. $\boxed{} + 4 = 12$

5. $9 + 6 = \boxed{}$

6. $8 + \boxed{} = 16$

7. $4 + \boxed{} = 11$

8. $\boxed{} + 7 = 10$

9. $5 + 8 = \boxed{}$

10. $9 + \boxed{} = 18$

Colour in your score

Test 23

Test 24 Shapes

These shapes have a line of **symmetry**.

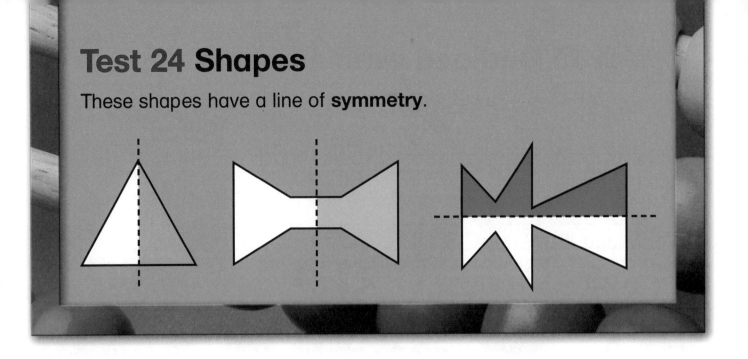

Draw the lines of symmetry on these shapes.

1.

2.

3.

4.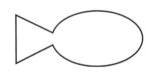

5.

Name these shapes.
Tick them if they are symmetrical.

6.
_____ ☐

7.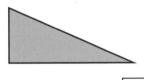
_____ ☐

8.
_____ ☐

9.
_____ ☐

10.
_____ ☐

10
9
8
7
6
5
4
3
2
1

Colour in your score

Test 24

Test 25 Odd and even numbers

even	2	4	6	8	10	12	14	16

odd	1	3	5	7	9	11	13	15

Write the next even number.

1. 22 ☐

2. 28 ☐

3. 36 ☐

4. 44 ☐

5. 40 ☐

Write the next odd number.

6. 39 ☐

7. 41 ☐

8. 27 ☐

9. 35 ☐

10. 43 ☐

Colour in your score

Test 25

Test 26 Money and place value

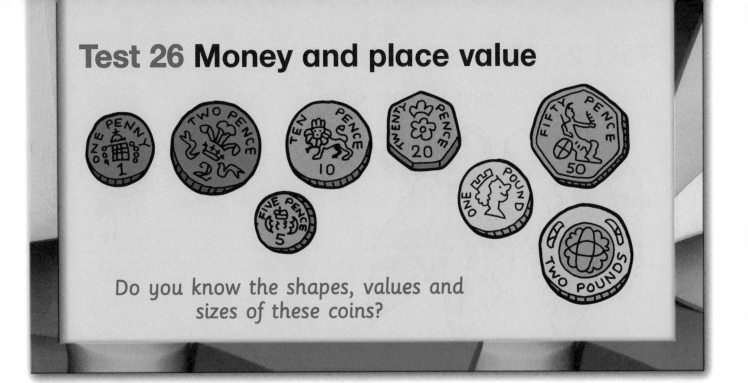

Do you know the shapes, values and sizes of these coins?

Write each of these totals.

1. 20p 20p 10p £1 ⇨ £ [.   ]

2. 50p 50p 20p 10p ⇨ £ [.   ]

3. 20p 20p 50p £1 ⇨ £ [.   ]

4. £1 £1 20p 10p ⇨ £ [.   ]

5. £1 50p 20p 10p ⇨ £ [.   ]

6. £1 £2 20p 10p ⇨ £ [.   ]

7. 10p 20p 20p £2 ⇨ £ [.   ]

8. £2 £2 50p 20p ⇨ £ [.   ]

9. 50p 50p 20p £2 ⇨ £ [.   ]

10. 20p 50p £1 £1 ⇨ £ [.   ]

Colour in your score

Test 26

Test 27 10 times table

You need to know your **10 times table**.

How quickly can you answer these?

1. 4 × 10 = ☐

2. 10 × 3 = ☐

3. 7 × 10 = ☐

4. 1 × 10 = ☐

5. 5 × 10 = ☐

6. 10 × 6 = ☐

7. 10 × 2 = ☐

8. 8 × 10 = ☐

9. 10 × 10 = ☐

10. 9 × 10 = ☐

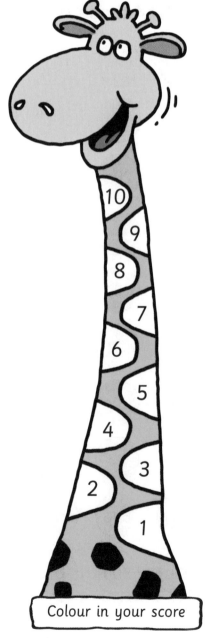

Colour in your score

Test 27

Test 28 Fractions of quantities

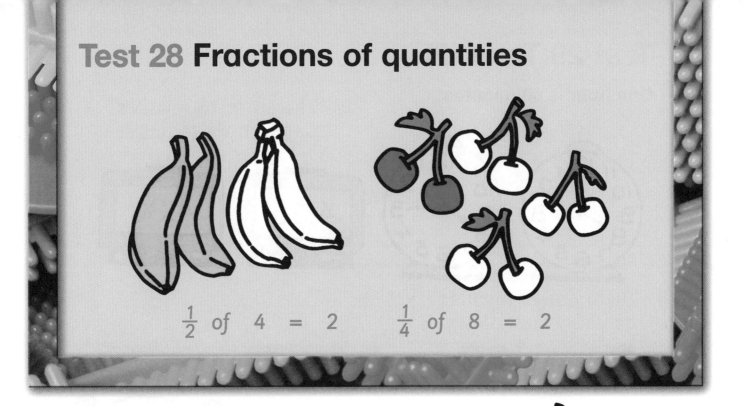

$\frac{1}{2}$ of 4 = 2 $\frac{1}{4}$ of 8 = 2

Find half of each of these.

1.  $\frac{1}{2}$ of 6 = ☐

2. $\frac{1}{2}$ of 10 = ☐

3.  $\frac{1}{2}$ of 12 = ☐

Work out the answers.

4. $\frac{1}{2}$ of 8 = ☐   8. $\frac{1}{4}$ of 12 = ☐

5. $\frac{1}{2}$ of 20 = ☐   9. $\frac{1}{2}$ of 18 = ☐

6. $\frac{1}{2}$ of 14 = ☐   10. $\frac{1}{4}$ of 4 = ☐

7. $\frac{1}{4}$ of 20 = ☐

Colour in your score

Test 29 Time (2)

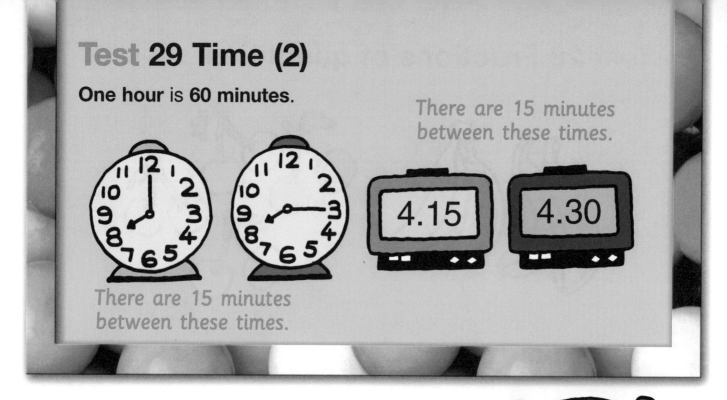

One hour is **60 minutes**.

There are 15 minutes between these times.

There are 15 minutes between these times.

4.15   4.30

Write how many minutes there are between each of these times.

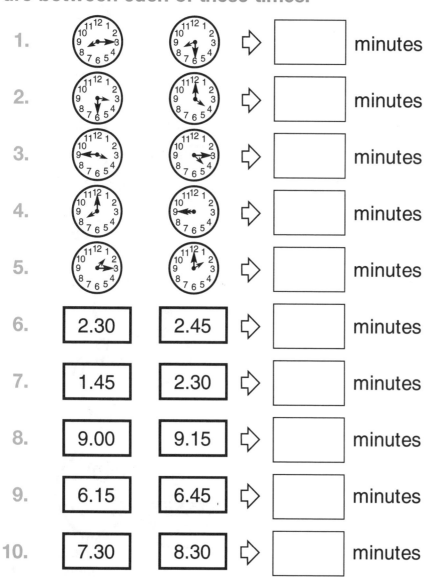

1. ⟹ [ ] minutes

2. ⟹ [ ] minutes

3. ⟹ [ ] minutes

4. ⟹ [ ] minutes

5. ⟹ [ ] minutes

6. | 2.30 | | 2.45 | ⟹ [ ] minutes

7. | 1.45 | | 2.30 | ⟹ [ ] minutes

8. | 9.00 | | 9.15 | ⟹ [ ] minutes

9. | 6.15 | | 6.45 | ⟹ [ ] minutes

10. | 7.30 | | 8.30 | ⟹ [ ] minutes

Colour in your score

Test 29

Test 30 Data: tables

This **table** shows the colours of children's tops.

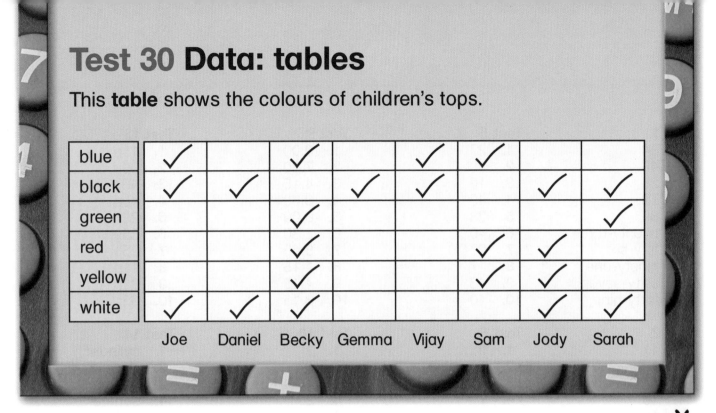

	Joe	Daniel	Becky	Gemma	Vijay	Sam	Jody	Sarah
blue	✓		✓		✓	✓		
black	✓	✓		✓	✓		✓	✓
green			✓					✓
red			✓			✓	✓	
yellow			✓			✓	✓	
white	✓	✓	✓				✓	✓

Look at the table and answer these questions.

1. Who has the most colours in their top? _____

2. Who has a black and white top? _____

3. What colours are in Sam's top? _____

4. Who has green in their top? _____

5. Who has no black in their top? _____

6. How many have white in their top? _____

7. How many have no blue in their top? _____

8. How many have 3 colours in their top? _____

9. Who has a single coloured top? _____

10. Who has no black or white in their top? _____

Colour in your score

ANSWERS

Test 1
1. 34
2. 46
3. 28
4. 72
5. 89
6. twenty-three
7. fifty-six
8. ninety-one
9. sixty-seven
10. forty-nine

Test 2
1. 11
2. 14
3. 14
4. 16
5. 14
6. 17
7. 16
8. 12
9. 18
10. 19

Test 3
1. 62p
2. 19p
3. 33p
4. 82p
5. 18p
6. 73p
7. 54p
8. 28p
9. 86p
10. 39p

Test 4
1. 3
2. 6
3. 5
4. 8
5. 4
6. quadrilateral/ square
7. pentagon
8. triangle
9. hexagon
10. rectangle/ quadrilateral

Test 5
1. 27
2. 39
3. 18
4. 42
5. 33
6. 40
7. 27
8. 17
9. 43
10. 40

Test 6
1. 3
2. 6
3. 5
4. 7
5. 5
6. 5
7. 2
8. 6
9. 4
10. 5

Test 7
1. 6
2. 8
3. 9
4. 10
5. 12
6. 4
7. 15
8. 15
9. 8
10. 6

Test 8
1. 6
2. 2
3. 2
4. 5
5. 3
6. 4
7. 2
8. 3
9. 3
10. 4

Test 9
1. 9.00
2. 7.30
3. 4.15
4. 3.30
5. 8.00
6. 2.30
7. 8.45
8. 1.15
9. 4.45
10. 3.15

Test 10
1. 1
2. 5
3. 4
4. 2
5. grapes
6. apples
7. 3
8. 3
9. 4
10. 17

Test 11
1. 40
2. 6
3. 9
4. 60
5. 20
6. 6
7. 80
8. 70
9. 2
10. 90

Test 12
1. 3
2. 8
3. 4
4. 9
5. 3
6. 6
7. 10
8. 5
9. 5
10. 7

Test 13
1. 15p
2. 30p
3. 45p
4. 40p
5. 20p
6. 55p
7. 25p
8. 11p
9. 22p
10. 33p

Test 14
1. cylinder
2. cone
3. cuboid
4. sphere
5. pyramid
6. cube
7. 5
8. 5
9. 6
10. 6

Test 15
1. 28
2. 44
3. 45
4. 30
5. 28
6. 16
7. 30
8. 15
9. 12
10. 30

Test 16
1. 60
2. 60
3. 40
4. 100
5. 90
6. 40
7. 60
8. 10
9. 30
10. 50